Wigan *Past*

WIGAN The voice of Wigan for 154 years
Observer

at heart publications

Wigan Past has been compiled by the *Wigan Observer's* Deputy Chief Photographer, **Frank Orrell**.

Frank started his career working in the darkroom of the Evening Post and Chronicle, which later became the *Wigan Evening Post*. After four years he became a photographer and has been taking photographs for Wigan's newspapers for 36 years.

Frank is married with two grown-up sons and one grandson.

First published in 2007 by
At Heart Ltd, 32 Stamford Street, Altrincham, Cheshire, WA14 1EY
in conjunction with
Wigan Observer, Martland Mill Lane, Wigan, WN5 0LX

ISBN: 978-1-84547-184-2

Printed by Bell & Bain Ltd, Glasgow.

Market Place, Wigan, in 1913.

Contents

Introduction   4

Around Wigan   5

Famous Visitors   30

Wigan at Work   39

Sport   59

Leisure   75

When we were young   99

Introduction

TAKE A step back in time courtesy of the photographic archives of the *Wigan Observer*. This magnificent collection of pictures, taken over many years by our photographers, unearths hidden secrets from times past.

These pages reveal many facets of Wigan's rich heritage – its wonderful people, magnificent buildings, celebrity visitors and famous sporting tradition.

Many faces, young and old, beam from the pages, enjoying their small moment of fame in front of the camera. The people of Wigan make the town what it is today, and their wide variety of experiences are reflected in this book.

Remember your school days or your time as a teenager? One image can take your mind right back to days long gone. That's why these beautiful images are so valuable – the perfect reminder of a different life.

Many of the buildings featured are long gone, but how our pictures will bring back memories – many happy, some sad.

Areas of the town have changed beyond recognition, but they are still very vivid in our minds.

Each picture will mean something different to each person, many of them personal recollections of very public moments.

We pay tribute to the men and women who have contributed to the area's thriving amateur sports scene and give them the chance to once again have their moment of glory – for everyone else to share!

Take time to browse through these pages and enjoy seeing for yourself just what makes Wigan the wonderful place it is now – and always has been.

Around Wigan

HERE we visit the landmarks of Wigan; places that are immediately recognisable, even though the photographs may have been taken decades ago. Town centre vistas, like those around Market Place; the view from Millgate; and images of shoppers walking up Standishgate, all hold a special magic for Wiganers.

But there are other landmarks, many long gone, that are just as fascinating, like the corner shop on Warrington Lane, the canal at Crook, Billinge Beacon, and the Bee Hive pub. These are little slices of our town that will bring back memories for some, and an insight into Wigan's past for others.

■ Market Place, Wigan, around the turn of the century.

■ The east side of Market Place, around 1861.

■ Market Place, Wigan, in 1950.

■ The changing face of Wigan Market Place. The view is from one of the stores in the early 1970s.

■ Market Place in the mid-seventies.

■ Wigan Market Place in the 1970s.

■ The old Wigan Market Square in the early 1970s. Cars were allowed to park on the cobbled square and the nearby bus station was always a hive of activity.

■ An alleyway off Market Place with the Old Dog Inn and music hall on the left at the beginning of the 20th century.

■ The Mayor of Wigan, Councillor Jimmy Jones, cuts the cord to officially open the new Wigan market hall in 1987.

■ The old Wigan market hall.

■ A view from the civic centre of the top end of Millgate when demolition was taking place near the Wiend in 1977.

■ A building known as Well's House on Millgate.

■ A little girl minds the pram outside Whelan's supermarket on Mesnes Street in the early 1970s.

■ The Bee Hive pub on Wigan Lane in the early 1900s.

■ Memories of author George Orwell, who wrote *The Road to Wigan Pier* after visiting the town in 1936, come flooding back with this picture taken at the junction of Warrington Lane and Sovereign Road in 1972. Orwell lodged nearby.

■ The Bird i'th Hand pub, or 'Hen Hole' as it was locally known, on Gidlow Lane at the beginning of the 20th century.

■ A resident of Bird Street in Ince pauses from her sweeping chores in the 1960s.

■ A scene from 1900 showing the Douglas Tavern at the corner of Chapel Lane and Douglas Street.

■ Part of the old St John's School which was demolished to make way for North Way in Wigan town centre in the 1970s.

■ The Bird i'th Hand Inn at Hindley, with Proe and Co. coffin-makers next door.

■ The Coop's building on Dorning Street with Crawford Street police station on the right in the early part of the 20th century.

■ Wigan Infirmary from the air with Wigan Lane on the right in the early part of the 20th century.

■ The Wigan Bank for Savings, pictured here in the early 1900s, was a dispensary in earlier times.

■ Dean's paperhanging shop with John S. Rattray's photographers in Wigan at the turn of the century.

■ The Wigan Pier area in 1939 with Pottery Road and Eckersley Mill in the background.

■ The top end of Standishgate leading out of Wigan at the beginning of the 20th century.

Above and below: Little London, off Standishgate, in the late 1800s.

■ Standishgate, in 1939.

■ The old doctor's surgery building at the junction of High Street and School Lane, Standish, in 1980 where Subway and the Spar supermarket are now located.

■ The Wheatsheaf Hotel and the old Almond's Brewery building at the junction of Preston Road and School Lane, Standish, in the early 1980s. Somerfield supermarket is now situated here.

■ When winters were winters and snow storms were more common than nowadays. Traffic chaos caused by a heavy snowfall on Standishgate in Wigan town centre in 1984.

■ The Wheatsheaf Hotel and the old Almond's Brewery building on the left at the crossroads of Preston Road, High Street, Market Street and School Lane, Standish, in the early 1980s.

■ Broad O'th Lane, Shevington, in the early part of the 20th century.

■ *Left and below:*
Scholes in the 1960s, as
the terraced houses
were demolished to
make way for the flats
and maisonettes.

■ A house-proud woman cleans her front step watched by two little boys in Stanley Street, Scholes, in 1969.

■ Villagers on the coal tipper to the Leeds and Liverpool Canal in Crooke Village.

■ A busy day on the Leeds-Liverpool Canal near Chapel Lane in 1963. The canal was always busy in those days and there was little room for pleasure craft.

■ The Old Cottages on Ladies Lane, Hindley, in the early 1900s, with one of the area's many pits in the background.

■ Pemberton soon after the turn of the century, with a view looking from White Street across Ormskirk Road and into Fleet Street.

■ Westwood Power Station and its smoking chimneys in the 1980s.

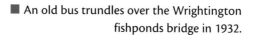

■ An old bus trundles over the Wrightington fishponds bridge in 1932.

Famous Visitors

WHO'D have thought the likes of Arnold Schwarzeneggar and soul legend Geno Washington would be snapped in Wigan? From official royal and government visits to celebrity appearances and on-stage performances, here we look at some of the famous faces that we have welcomed to our town over the years..

■ Miss Great Britain Kathleen Winstanley, Arnold Schwarzenegger and friend pictured outside Kath's home in Kitt Green in 1968.

■ The Prince of Wales' visit to Wigan in July 1921.

■ The Queen Mother in Wigan in June 1959.

■ A royal visit by Queen Elizabeth II in 1954 to open Wigan Technical College.

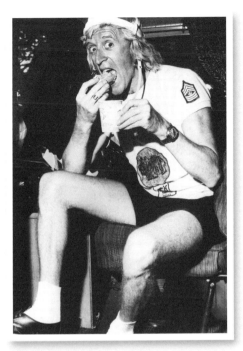

■ Jimmy Savile during a break in Standish on one of his Lands End to John O' Groats bike rides in the early 1970s.

■ Geno Washington with a friend backstage at Wigan Casino in the early 1970s.

■ Long John Baldry on stage at Wigan Casino in the early 1970s.

■ The Equals with Eddie Grant backstage at Wigan Casino in the 1970s.

■ Charttoppers Amen Corner on stage at Wigan Casino in the early 1970s.

■ Popular local band Harlem John's Reshuffle on stage at Wigan Casino in the 1970s.

■ Top musicians Georgie Fame and Alan Price as they appeared in Scholes to open a shop in the early 1970s.

■ Page three girl Sam Fox with race winners at Standish Carnival in 1985.

■ Television star Gary Wilmot crowns the carnival queen at Standish Carnival in 1985.

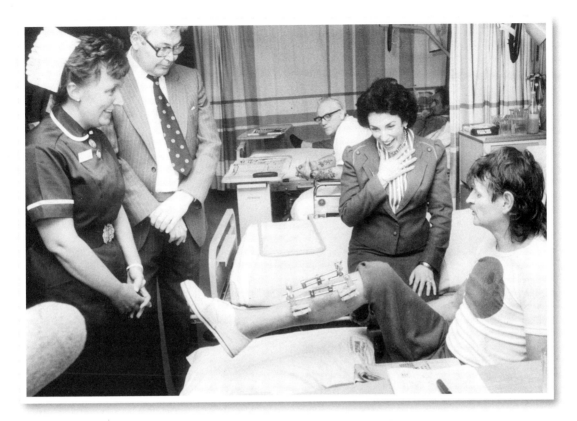

■ MP Edwina Currie touring the wards after opening an Acute Unit at Wigan Infirmary in April 1987.

■ Duncan Goodhew splashes out with multiple sclerosis sufferer, Muriel Williams, to launch a charity 'swimathon' at Wigan Baths in the 1980s.

■ Ken Dodd with fans as he opens the newly refurbished Makinson Arcade in the 1980s.

■ It's the 1980s and cricket ace Clive Lloyd visits the town to help fundraising at Wigan Hospice.

Wigan at Work

FROM the black-faced colliers who worked down the pit to the nurses with their starched uniforms at the new Wigan Infirmary, this is Wigan at work.

These pictures actually show parts of Wigan being created - like the council workmen who are shown creating Plank Street in Wigan and demolishing the old chimney at Billinge Hospital - as well as institutions like the old Marks and Spencer store in Makinson Arcade.

And then there are little glimpses of Wigan life: dinner being served in the Market Hotel, newspaper sellers in the town centre and staff at Bradley's Men's Outfitters.

■ Wigan girls in the huge drawing room of a local cotton mill.

■ Marks and Spencer's beginnings in Makinson Arcade, Wigan.

Marks and Spencer's store in Wigan in its early days.

■ The staff of Marks and Spencer's store in Makinson Arcade in 1925.

■ Council workmen on Plank Street, Wigan, in the 1920s.

Arthur and Lizzie Aspinall with assistants outside their grocer's shop in Shevington in 1924.

The old Lancashire Evening Post office in Powell Street in 1953.

■ The manager and his assistant of Bradley's Men's Outfitters on Market Street, Wigan, in 1967.

■ Dinner is served in the Market Hotel in Wigan in the early 1970s.

■ The trophy winning HJ Heinz fire brigade at Kitt Green in 1975.

■ Margaret's baby and children's wear stall in the Old Arcade, Wigan, in the early 1970s.

■ A menswear stall holder in the Old Arcade in the early 1970s.

■ Mary Davies in 1967 when she started at BHS in Wigan. She went on to become manager of the new store in the Grand Arcade.

■ The Mayor of Wigan, Councillor S. Taylor, unveils the plaque to open the new Pemberton Health Centre on May 3, 1967.

■ An impressive range of products were available from the new health centre.

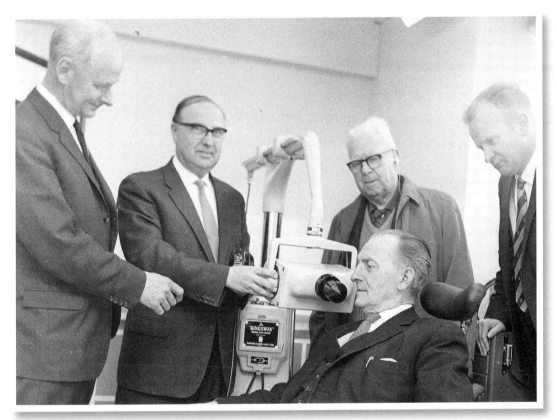

■ Trying out the medical equipment at the newly opened Pemberton Health Centre.

■ Nurses celebrate passing their SRN certificate in 1956.

■ The busy Wigan outside market in 1976.

■ Newspaper sellers in Wigan town centre in the early 1970s.

■ William Parr behind the family shop on Bridge Street in Hiindley in the 1950s.

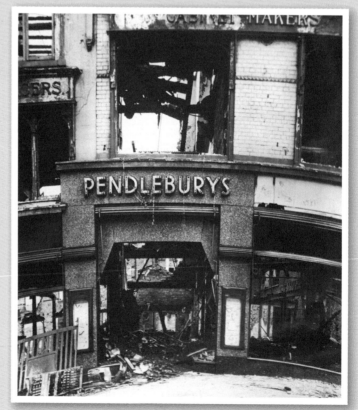

■ Workers at Coop's factory in Dorning Street, Wigan, have a special lunch to celebrate the Queen's Silver Jubilee in 1977.

■ The dilapidated Pendlebury's store after a fire in the 1950s. The store later became Debenhams.

■ Debenhams staff with Santa on a promotional barge trip in the 1980s.

■ Workmen demolishing a tall chimney at Billinge Hospital in the 1970s.

■ The plaque unveiling of the new intensive care unit at Wigan Infirmary by Dr. F.N. Marshall in May 1967.

■ Examining the specialised equipment in the newly opened intensive care unit at Wigan Infirmary in May 1967.

■ Nurses at work in the new intensive care unit at Wigan Infirmary.

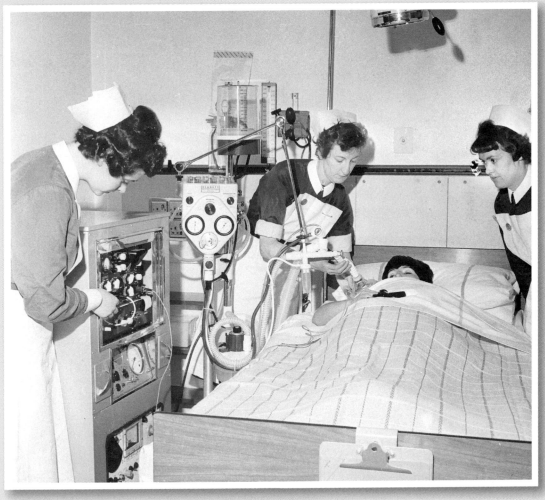

■ Old and young soldiers stand to attention at the Remembrance Day service near the Wigan War Memorial in the early 1970s.

■ James Berry outside his Foxfield Garage, Shevington, in the early 1970s.

■ Wigan coal miners pictured in 1910.

■ A Wigan miner's backyard amongst the slums of 1939.

■ Down the Victoria pit, Wigan in the early part of the 20th century.

■ Years later, the work was just as dirty but miners were at least provided with protective hard hats.

■ Pictured here in 1920, Pemberton Colliery was the first colliery in Lancashire to have the winding gear constructed from large iron girder frames.

■ Former employees at Westwood Power Station just prior to its closure in 1986.

■ Old Wigan Power Station built in 1900 at Westwood in Wigan. This picture shows the control room with Maurice Mason of Riverside Avenue, Whelley, whose son Keith submitted the photograph to us. Maurice had to manually switch Wigan's street lighting on when darkness fell in the days before automation.

■ Coal arrives to power the Old Wigan Power Station which was dismantled in the 1960s to make way for the modern Westwood power station.

Sport

WIGAN has always had a rich history of sporting heritage and is known across the globe for its professional rugby and football teams. But the town also boasts a wide range of skilful, enthusiastic and varied amateur sports people.

Each weekend thousands of people of all ages descend upon the parks and pitches across the borough to take part in rugby league, football and rugby union matches, and other popular sports. So, this chapter is a celebration of Wigan's strong sporting heritage, and all the athletes, bowlers, anglers and boxers, young and old, who have trained and competed, and joined together for a weekly dose of friendly rivalry over the years.

■ Wigan Boys in 1949 brimming with pride after winning another trophy. Photo supplied by Mr T. Moore of Marus Bridge.

■ Warrington Lane Boys in 1951.

■ Picture shows, we believe, Highfield Rugby Club in 1926.

■ Whelley St Stephen's from the 1922/23 season. The photo was supplied by Brian Barker of Whitley whose late father Ellis Barker captained the side, and is seen here holding the medals.

Former Mayor of Wigan, Bernard Coyle, pictured, front left, with a cup-winning St Patrick's rugby team at Central Park in 1942. Pictured are (back row): T. Moran, J. O'Shea, J. McGurrin, K Farrell, J. Connor, M.Moran, R.Livesey, F. Moran. (middle row): T. McDonnell, J. Tinsley, W. Lowe, E. Toohey, E. Eccleston, J. McGurrin, W. Woosey. (sitting): J. McDonnell, B. Coyle, F. Keenan, T. Conway.

■ Orrell RUFC 1st XV in 1950 sent in by Robert Falla, midde row, left, who played centre quarter.

■ A muddy afternoon at Edge Hall Road as Orrell do battle in a line-out in the 1970s.

■ Action from a Wigan Rugby Union Club match in the 1970s.

■ Happy faces welcome Wigan Rugby League team home to Central Park after winning the Challenge Cup in 1988.

■ Whelley Secondary Modern at Central Park.

■ Former Wigan Athletic, Everton and Nottingham Forest star, Duncan McKenzie, starts a 10-mile run from Orrell Rugby Union Club in 1980.

■ Some of the 670 runners at the start of the 1977 Wigan Six Road Race turn the bend out of Mesnes Street into Standishgate.

■ Winner of the 1977 Wigan Six Road Race, Geoff Smith, crosses the finishing line on the Market Square.

■ Runners in the 1983 Wigan Six Road Race set off along Northway.

■ The old Woodhouse Stadium Athletics Ground photographed in 1975.

■ Young Wigan wrestlers in action in the 1970s.

■ Encouragement for the young Wigan wrestlers from their handlers.

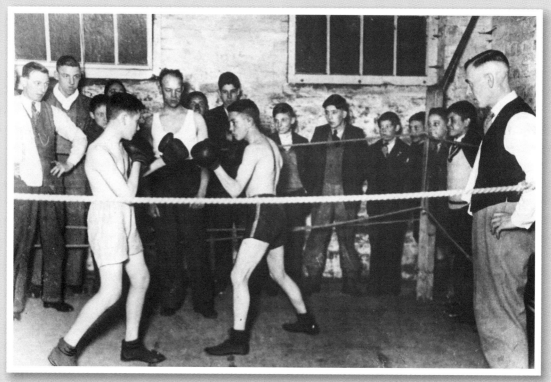

■ In the ring at Wigan Boys' Club, Clayton Street, in 1936.

■ Young cricketers get some advice from Wigan Cricket Club stalwart Frank Layland at Bull Hey in the early 1970s.

■ Wigan karate expert Billy Higgins in action smashing tiles in the 1980s.

■ Karting at the Three Sisters Race Track in the 1970s.

■ A stage of the Lombard RAC Rally which roared through the grounds of Haigh Hall in the 1980s.

■ The Navigation pub's angling team, Gathurst, with trophies in the 1940s.

■ The bowling team from the Hesketh Arms, Shevington Moor, in 1933.

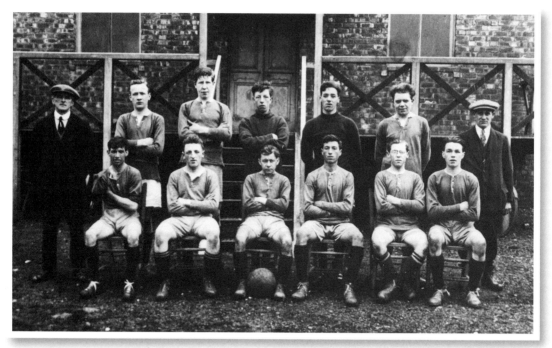

■ Shevington football team in 1922.

■ Shevington football team for the 1929-30 season with keen player, vicar Rev. Samuel Crabtree, front row, third left.

■ Appley Bridge AFC team for the 1919-20 season.

■ Hindley Youth Service line up after winning the Howarth Shield in 1943. The players were given photographs due to a shortage of medals during the war. Photo supplied by Henry Parr of Hindley.

■ Almond Brook Celtic
FC winning the Amateur
Shield in 1969-70. Photo
supplied by Mr Holmes of
Newtown.

■ The trophy winning
Timberlakes football
team in the early 1970s.

Leisure

WIGANERS certainly know how to have a good time. From celebrating the royal jubilees of 1935 and 1977, to get-togethers at the Comet Youth Club and Walking Days, we certainly know how to throw a party.

These pictures chronicle some of the clubs, pubs and societies that we have spent our leisure time over the years, as well as some more intimate shots – like the couple preparing for their tandem bicycle ride, and friends enjoying themselves in the Empress Ballroom.

■ Ladies from Ashton leave from Princess Road on a charabanc trip in the early 1900s.

■ Playing quoits on the Wigan Boys' Club own barge *Duke of Gloucester* at Skipton (Leeds-Liverpool Canal) on 2 August 1937.

■ Undated picture of walkers at the beacon building at the top of Billinge Hill.

■ One man and his dog in Borsdane Wood, Hindley, in the early part of the 20th century.

■ Shevington Mothers' Union dressed in period costume, photographed in the 1930s.

■ Racobite walks on Broad O'th Lane, Shevington, at the turn of the 20th century.

■ St John's bible class in 1926.

■ Four local gentleman outside of the Railway Hotel in Hindley in the first part of the 20th century. Photo supplied by Henry Parr of Hindley.

■ The band and local community gather outside Hindley Royal British Legion to raise the Union Flag. Second from right is William Parr, next to him is Sam Edwards. Photo supplied by Henry Parr of Hindley.

■ Air Training Corps on parade in Hindley in the 1940s. Wilfred Dickson (far right) inspects the troops. Photo supplied by Henry Parr of Hindley.

■ Wiganers celebrate the Jubilee
of George V in 1935.

■ Children in Gillan Road, Swinley, celebrating the Queen's Silver Jubilee in 1977.

■ A street party in Plane Avenue, Worsley Hall, to celebrate the Queen's Silver Jubilee.

■ Kiddies of Calder Avenue, Hindley Green, in fancy dress to celebrate the Queen's Silver Jubilee.

■ Henry Parr with his wife Ivy on their tandem after the war.

■ Youngsters enjoying themselves at a Hindley dance in the 1950s.

■ Wigan Casino on a Sunday night in the late 1960s with local group Harlem John's Reshuffle on stage.

■ New Year's Eve at Wigan Casino in 1969.

■ Friends enjoying themselves in Wigan's Empress Ballroom.

■ Wigan's Miss Great Britain winner, Kathleen Winstanley, presents a trophy to Kitt Green pensioners in 1970.

■ Kathleen Winstanley, during a visit to the Duke of Lancaster's Own Yeomanry A Squadron at the Drill Hall, Wigan, in 1972. The squadron adopted Kathleen as their pin-up.

■ Summer days at Haigh Country Park in 1984.

■ Fishing fun at Haigh Country Park in 1984.

■ Model boats attract the attention of young lads at Haigh in 1984.

■ Children enjoy a game of football watched by onlookers in the 1970s.

■ Entrants for a Wigan mother and baby competition in 1986.

■ A youngster queues with his mum for one of the famous Debenham sales in the 1960s.

■ Appley Bridge boat rally in 1977.

■ A lunchtime pint in the Market Hotel in Wigan in the early 1970s.

■ Walking Days used to be a feature of Wallgate. Here we see a procession of local Catholic gentlemen from around 1952.

■ Happy times for these young ladies at a Comet Youth Club fun day at Poolstock in 1978. Amongst the revellers are Carol Barker, Carol Vernon, Janet Gordon, Ann Hagerty, Ann Johnson, and Jeanette and Vivien Mahoney.

■ Eccentric smallholding farmer Derek Fuller, who had butting contests with his goat in the 1980s.

■ A husband and wife team from New Springs who won prizes for their horticultural skills in the 1980s.

■ Happy holidays in Norley Hall in the 1970s.

■ An aerial view of tents erected for Wigan Summer Show in Mesnes Park in the early 1970s.

■ A thirsty dog on a hot summer's day in 1976.

■ Youngsters help out Delmo Motor Salvage at Wigan Motor Show in 1983.

■ A real panda car at Wigan Motor Show in 1983.

■ Young lads meet Automan at Wigan Motor Show in 1984.

■ The scene at Wigan Motor Show in 1984.

■ An army motorcycle display team in action at a Wigan Carnival in the 1970s.

■ Members of the Comet Motorcycle Club in 1983.

■ Youngsters in Northumberland Street, Whelley, dress up to celebrate the Queen's Silver Jubilee in 1977.

When we were young

THESE terrific pictures will bring back plenty of memories for the young people featured. Whether your schooldays are a long and distant memory or just a few years ago, we all remember having the classroom photograph taken. But can you still remember those who lined up alongside you? And what about all the fun you had outside of school. These pictures offer a glimpse of the days when we were carefree and full of fun.

■ Three boys and a dog race along the street in Bradley Village in the 1970s.

■ All wrapped up for some fun in the snow at Haigh Hall in the early 1980s.

■ Walking Day in Hindley in the 1950s.

■ An idyllic scene with young friends on a sandy beach, with a moored boat and swans gliding by on Scotman's Flash off Poolstock Lane in 1953. Enjoying the day are Mary Heathcote, Sheila Adcock, Barbara Wright, Mavis Foster and Pat and Kathleen Wright.

■ Two guides from the 1940s.

■ Local guides in Wigan in 1911.

■ Wigan's girl guides on parade in the 1950s.

■ Young lads in Norley Hall with their puppy in the 1970s.

■ Children have a splashing time during summer holidays in the 1982.

■ A little girl has a surprise encounter with a diver at Wigan Boat Rally in 1983.

■ A game of baseball for youngsters on a summer's day in the 1970s.

■ Enthusiastic competitors in the sack race at Beech Hill Primary School sports day in the early 1970s.

A bespectacled young footballer shows his skills in the 1970s.

Match of the Day at St Bernadette's RC Primary School, Shevington, in 1986.

■ Muddy marvels. A couple of young lads after a muddy game of football in the 1980s.

■ Football fun for Shevington children in the early 1980s.

■ Shevington children build a giant snowman in 1984.

■ Clowning around 1980s-style at Standish Library with children's entertainer, Terry De Maxin.

■ Dan Dan the Magic Man entertains children and parents at the Buck's Head pub, Abram, in 1985.

■ Magician Fred Barton entertains children at Hindley Library in 1985.

■ Nurses with young patients at Wigan Infirmary in 1967.

■ Children on the skyrocket play equipment near the Brookhouse flats in Scholes in the early 1970s.

■ Clarinet prizewinners Joanne Young and Rachael Lowe, during the 1984 Wigan Schools Music Festival.

■ *Opposite page, top:* Prizewinners during the Wigan Schools' Music Festival in 1984.

■ *Opposite page, bottom:* The cast of the Christmas production at St Mark's School, Newtown, in 1968.

■ Julia Wilkinson, Caroline Wilcock and Mark Westhead who were in good voice during the Wigan Schools' Music Festival in 1984.

St Luke's School, Orrell, in 1909.

■ Shevington Primary School children in 1948.

■ Highfield St Matthew's in June 1960.

■ Form 3C at John Rigby Grammar School, Orrell, in 1963.

■ Senior and Junior pupils from Gidlow Secondary Modern School who swept the board to win all the trophies for the girls during the 1951 inter-schools athletics event.

■ All Saints cup winning football team in 1934. (back row, left-right): Mr Scarborough, Mr Dowling, Mr Moorfield. Also on the picture are Knowles, Spencer, Ainscough, Collier, Williams, McGee, Ball, Ashurst, Highway and Henry Parr (bottom right).

■ Hindley Argyle Street School's football team, pictured in 1957.

■ St Joseph's rugby team in 1937.